Wildlife
in the CITY

Abandoned and Escaped Animals

Rachel Eagen

Author: Rachel Eagen

Editorial director: Kathy Middleton

Art director: Rosie Gowsell Pattison

Editor: Petrice Custance

Proofreader: Wendy Scavuzzo

**Production coordinator and
 Prepress technician:** Ken Wright

Print coordinator: Katherine Berti

Images

Shutterstock.com: Thacho_kl: p28
(top right)

All other images
from Shutterstock

Produced for Crabtree Publishing
by Plan B Book Packagers
www.planbbookpackagers.com

Library and Archives Canada Cataloguing in Publication

Title: Abandoned and escaped animals / Rachel Eagen.
Names: Eagen, Rachel, 1979- author.
Description: Series statement: Wildlife in the city | Includes index.
Identifiers: Canadiana (print) 20190128283 |
  Canadiana (ebook) 20190128291 |
  ISBN 9780778766865 (hardcover) |
  ISBN 9780778766964 (softcover) |
  ISBN 9781427124135 (HTML)
Subjects: LCSH: Feral animals—Juvenile literature. | LCSH: Introduced
  animals—Juvenile literature. | LCSH: Urban ecology (Sociology)—
  Juvenile literature. | LCSH: Human-animal relationships. |
  LCSH: Nature—Effect of human beings on—Juvenile literature.
Classification: LCC SF140.F47 E24 2019 | DDC j591.6/2—dc23

Library of Congress Cataloging-in-Publication Data

CIP available at the Library of Congress

LCCN: 2019023698

Crabtree Publishing Company

www.crabtreebooks.com   1-800-387-7650

Printed in the U.S.A./102019/CG20190809

**Published in Canada
Crabtree Publishing**
616 Welland Ave.
St. Catharines, Ontario
L2M 5V6

**Published in the United States
Crabtree Publishing**
PMB 59051
350 Fifth Avenue, 59th Floor
New York, New York 10118

**Published in the United Kingdom
Crabtree Publishing**
Maritime House
Basin Road North, Hove
BN41 1WR

**Published in Australia
Crabtree Publishing**
Unit 3–5 Currumbin Court
Capalaba
QLD 4157

CONTENTS

FERAL ON THE FRINGE 4

HOME HABITAT 6

LIFE ON THE STREETS.. 8

HERE, KITTY, KITTY 10

URBAN PRESSURE 12

FERAL FIDO 14

CULLS AND CONTROVERSY.................................... 16

SOOOO-EY!... 18

SLITHER AND SCATTER... 20

ATTACK OF THE KILLER...GOLDFISH? 22

INVADERS AND GRAZERS....................................... 24

PIGEON POWER 26

FERALS AROUND THE WORLD.................................. 28

LEARNING MORE 30

GLOSSARY 31

INDEX AND QUESTIONS & ANSWERS 32

FERAL ON THE FRINGE

"Hissss! Snarrrl! Mee-OWWW!" In the dark of night, while we snooze in soft beds, the neighborhood comes alive. Hungry cats prowl the streets. Stray dogs skulk in the shadows of alleys, knocking over trash cans and sniffing at **roadkill**. On the surface, cities seem to be spaces just for people. For centuries, we humans have designed and built them to suit our needs. But **urban** spaces also crawl with many **species** of animals—including those that were once pets.

It is estimated that there are more than 100 million feral cats around the world.

In the U.S., feral and outdoor cats kill up to 3.7 billion birds each year.

PETS TO PACKS

Domesticated animals depend on humans to feed, shelter, and care for them. Pets such as cats and dogs are examples of domesticated animals. Feral animals were once domesticated, but now fend for themselves. Some ferals have been abandoned by their owners, while others have escaped. Life as a feral or stray is tough. Food can be hard to find, and there are other dangers such as disease.

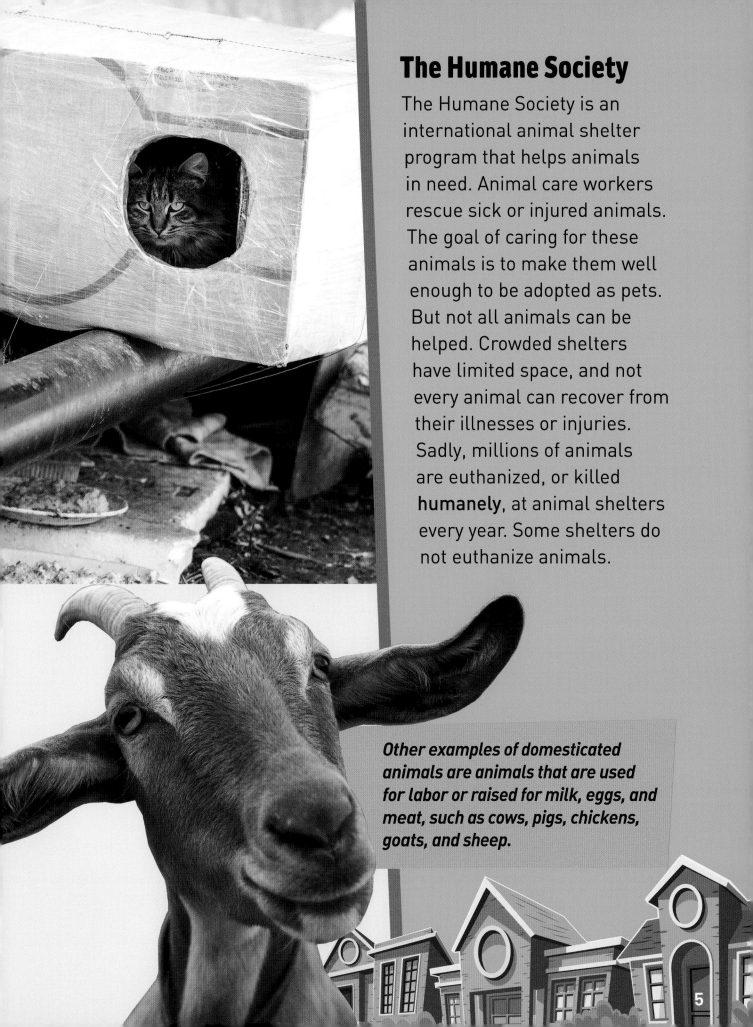

The Humane Society

The Humane Society is an international animal shelter program that helps animals in need. Animal care workers rescue sick or injured animals. The goal of caring for these animals is to make them well enough to be adopted as pets. But not all animals can be helped. Crowded shelters have limited space, and not every animal can recover from their illnesses or injuries. Sadly, millions of animals are euthanized, or killed **humanely**, at animal shelters every year. Some shelters do not euthanize animals.

Other examples of domesticated animals are animals that are used for labor or raised for milk, eggs, and meat, such as cows, pigs, chickens, goats, and sheep.

HOME HABITAT

Strays are cats and dogs that have lived with or around people at some point. They may have been pets that slipped out the door and got lost. Or they may have been abandoned by their humans. Unlike strays, ferals are not used to living with people as pets. Strays are more likely to be friendlier to humans.

Some people leave out food for stray cats and dogs. This can attract mice and rats.

Feral dogs and cats hunt backyard wildlife, including birds, rabbits, and rodents such as mice and squirrels.

Stray dogs shelter in alleys, under cars, and in abandoned buildings.

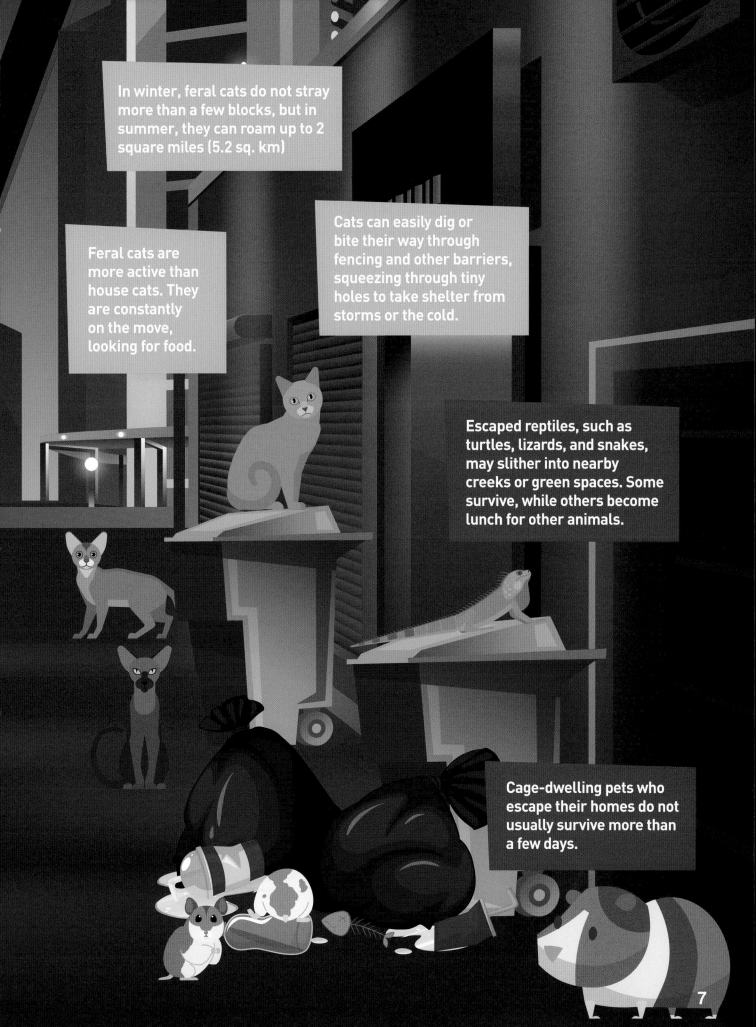

In winter, feral cats do not stray more than a few blocks, but in summer, they can roam up to 2 square miles (5.2 sq. km)

Feral cats are more active than house cats. They are constantly on the move, looking for food.

Cats can easily dig or bite their way through fencing and other barriers, squeezing through tiny holes to take shelter from storms or the cold.

Escaped reptiles, such as turtles, lizards, and snakes, may slither into nearby creeks or green spaces. Some survive, while others become lunch for other animals.

Cage-dwelling pets who escape their homes do not usually survive more than a few days.

LIFE ON THE STREETS

Feral and stray animals have harder, shorter lives than the average household pet. They must constantly look for food and water, eating whatever they can find. Hungry animals are expert dumpster divers, but garbage food can make them sick. Feral cats and small dogs often become meals for stronger animals such as coyotes.

Have you ever noticed a tailless or three-legged stray in your neighborhood? Many ferals lose limbs through accidents, such as getting hit by cars or falling out of trees or off rooftops. Frostbitten ears are also common.

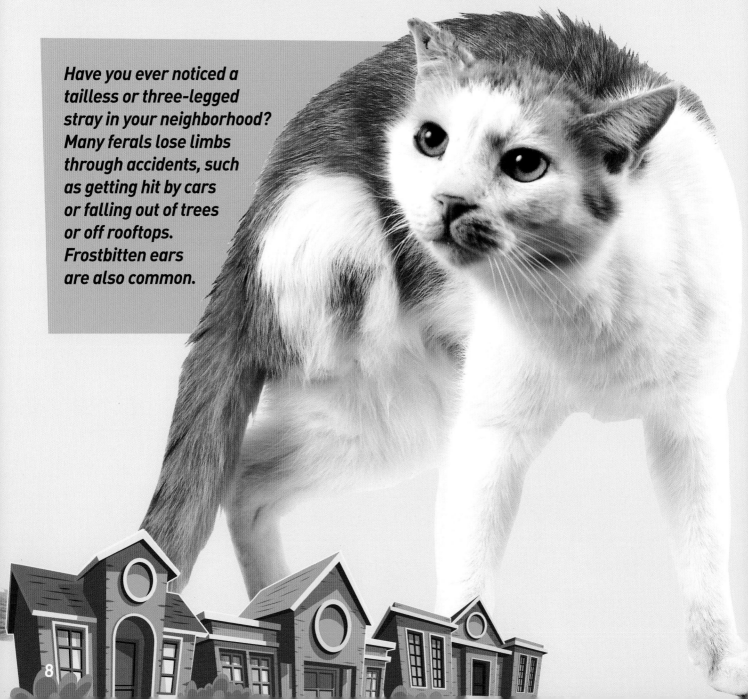

OL' SCARFACE

Injuries are common for ferals. When you are fighting for scraps on the street, it's easy to lose an ear or an eye. Many humans views strays and ferals as a **nuisance**. They damage property and use parks and backyards as toilets. Unlike their house-pet cousins, they have never had shots that protect them from certain diseases. Feral cats can spread diseases, such as toxoplasmosis. This is caused by a **parasite** found in cat poop. Some people use cruel methods for getting rid of feral animals. Many ferals are shot, poisoned, trapped, or drowned.

This feral, or street dog, has mange. It is a skin disease caused by mites *and it causes hair loss and itching. Many ferals also suffer from fleas, ticks, and worms.*

This dog's ear is a feast for ticks.

HERE, KITTY, KITTY

Cats are skilled hunters. They crouch low to the ground, the soft pads of their paws allowing them to silently creep up on their prey.

Feral cats often live in a group, or colony. In colonies, they defend their territory together, to protect their supply of food and water. Feral cats are often afraid of people. They are nocturnal, or night-prowling animals.

Cats are fearless at navigating rooftops and fences. This is partly due to their tails, which give them great balance as well as the ability to change direction quickly.

Feral cats use their strong back legs to pounce and their front claws to grab their victims. Cat attacks are the most common causes of injury for animals brought into wildlife hospitals.

Cats also use their tails to communicate. Slow, gentle movement signals affection or a request to play, while a quick flicking motion means LEAVE ME ALONE. A fluffy, lowered tail indicates fear.

A cat's whiskers are the same width as its body. They help cats sense things around them.

Even though feral cats live outdoors on their own, people sometimes take care of feral colonies. They feed them, and get them **spayed** or **neutered**, and **vaccinated** against diseases. The American Society for the Prevention of Cruelty to Animals (ASPCA) calls these animals community cats.

A cat's tongue is covered in tiny barbs, or hooks that curl toward its throat. These help a cat to groom itself, working like a comb as it licks its fur.

Cats have excellent eyesight and can see well at night. When a cat looks into bright light, its pupils narrow into thin slits.

Muscles in a cat's throat and vocal cords work together to create purring. Mothers purr to guide their blind, newborn kittens to nurse. Kittens learn to purr when they are two days old.

URBAN PRESSURE

Not all animals can survive in the wild, but some species can turn feral quite easily. They quickly learn what to eat, where to shelter, and what dangers they need to avoid. Animals who succeed as feral species are those who can survive harsh weather and reproduce, or have babies. But success as a feral can create challenges for others.

Some feral animals that have been spayed or neutered and returned to the streets have an ear tipped. Ear tipping is a humane surgical removal of the tip of one ear. It identifies the animal and prevents it from being picked up as a stray.

Feral guinea pigs in Oahu harm the ecosystem.

ATTACK OF THE GUINEA PIG!

On the Hawaiian island of Oahu, feral guinea pigs eat **native** plants, including many that are **endangered**. Native to South America, these hungry fur-balls are thought to be the offspring of escaped pets. The guinea pigs do not have any natural **predators** and females give birth twice a year. In Oahu, they are considered an invasive species. An invasive species is a plant or animal that did not **originate** in the environment it currently lives. Some of the guinea pigs were caught and given homes at an **animal sanctuary**.

International Street Dog Foundation

The International Street Dog Foundation (ISDF) is a volunteer organization that helps street dogs around the world. Their international adoption program sends **rehabilitated** dogs to adoptive families. Some of the dogs have been saved from the dog meat trade in Asia. Others received treatment for bad injuries or illnesses. The foundation also helps animals who have been lost or abandoned because of a natural disaster, such as a hurricane or an earthquake.

FERAL FIDO

Feral dogs are called many names, such as stray, free-ranging, and street dogs. They depend on humans for food and shelter, but they avoid people as much as possible due to fear.

Dogs use their tails to communicate to other dogs, people, and other animals. They do not wag their tails when they are alone.

Most feral dogs live close to cities, eating food from garbage. Feral dogs have not been socialized by living with people. They may attack when they feel threatened.

A low-wagging tail indicates stress, and a tail that is tucked between the hind legs shows fear or submissiveness. Tails also help dogs to keep their balance, especially when climbing, running, turning, leaping, and swimming.

Dogs often lick their paws to groom. For a street dog, they may eat what is hiding between those toes, including roundworms, whipworms, tapeworms, and hookworms. These can cause disease.

Dogs have sweat glands on their noses and paw pads. When they are nervous, they will leave wet footprints where they walk.

Feral dogs often carry fleas that can carry disease and spread to other animals.

Panting helps dogs to cool down. They cannot sweat like humans do, but panting allows them to circulate air through their bodies. Panting can also mean that a dog is sick, stressed out, or in pain.

Dogs have excellent eyesight. They have large pupils that absorb light even in the dark. They also have a wide field of vision. They can see sharply from a distance.

A dog that has been abandoned by its owner will start to behave like a feral dog in about one month.

Real World

HAPPY FACTS

Love UnderDogs is a charity in the United Kingdom that rescues and finds homes for stray dogs from Romania. Since 2013, it has run a program to rescue dogs from the city of Brasov. The stray population used to be in the thousands. Love UnderDogs has helped reduce it to around 300.

CULLS AND CONTROVERSY

Wild hogs have gone hog wild in the southern United States and parts of central and western Canada. They strip grass from grasslands, and root through and destroy crops. They have caused more than $400 million in damages to farmland, parks, and even golf courses in the southern and central U.S. Feral hogs are among the feral animals that are captured or killed each year in North America.

Half of the wild hogs in the U.S. roam the state of Texas. The population is so high that the state has allowed people to hunt them all year, with no limit.

HUNTS AND ROUNDUPS

Texas has the largest feral hog population in the U.S.—with about two million. They are hunted to reduce the population. Some hunts are done from helicopters. The Humane Society opposes the helicopter hunts and believes there are other ways to manage the hogs, such as catching them with live traps. Feral horses and burros are another group of animals that threaten crops and **rangeland**. The U.S. Bureau of Land Management (BLM) oversees 27 million acres (11 million ha) of land where feral horses roam. Domesticated cattle also occupy the rangeland. The BLM rounds up horses and keeps them in holding pens.

Wild Horses of the Xeni Gwet'in

Around 2,000 feral horses live on the Elegesi Qayus Wild Horse Preserve in British Columbia, Canada. The land was established by the Xeni Gwet'in (honey gwe-teen) First Nations people, in an effort to protect this feral species. A ranger, appointed by the Xeni Gwet'in, patrols the preserve to make sure that the horses are healthy and unharmed. Wild horse tours are offered to help fund the preserve. Many Canadians are fighting to have the horses declared a **heritage species**, so that they will be protected outside of the preserve.

SOOOO-EY!

Feral hogs have long, bristly hairs all over their body. They can be black, red, brown, or mottled.

Adult feral hogs prefer their own company, but females travel in groups called sounders. These groups vary in size, from 2 to 20 sows and their piglets. Very large sounders may have up to 50 members.

Hogs are active at night, an ideal time to be rooting through gardens. They spend their days snoozing and hiding, making them harder for hunters to find.

A feral hog is a large animal with a barrel-shaped body, short legs, a long head, a short, thick neck, and a wet snout.

To avoid hunters, they can run 30 miles per hour (48.3 kph) in short bursts.

Wild hogs have four pointy toes on each foot, two front toes that are excellent for walking through mud, and two back toes located higher up, toward the ankle.

Wild hogs like to always live close to a water source, such as near rivers, lakes, and creeks.

Feral hogs are a tricky animal to hunt because they can hear hunters long before hunters see them, giving them plenty of time to escape.

Feral hogs are domesticated hogs that escaped or were set loose in the wild. They **adapted** well to living wild and are more muscular than domesticated hogs.

Hogs use their tusks to defend themselves in an attack, and to spear their enemies in a fight.

They use their powerful snouts to root, or push up soil, in search of insects, roots, and acorns. They also damage farm fields and eat crops.

SLITHER AND SCATTER

Forget cute and cuddly. Exotic pets, such as reptiles, spiders, and unusual birds, have exploded in popularity since the 1980s. Today, more than 500 species of birds and 500 species of reptiles are traded all over the world. Some are shipped to pet stores or exotic pet dealers to be sold to adventurous pet owners. Others are smuggled into countries illegally.

SNAKE ESCAPE

In North America, most of the exotic pets for sale in pet stores come from suppliers who specialize in **breeding** rare species. These animals sometimes escape their enclosures and head for the bright lights of the city— or a sewage system. Some of these pets are released into creeks, rivers, and **conservation** areas. In Florida, Burmese pythons released or escaped from their owners have established themselves as an invasive species. They have damaged wetland ecosystems in Florida, including the entire Everglades National Park.

Burmese pythons can grow up to 23 feet (7 m) long and weigh 200 pounds (91 kg). It is believed they have reduced the population of deer, red fox, and raccoons in the Everglades.

Look Around You: Exotic Pets in Your Pet Store

Ask an adult to take a trip with you to your local pet store. What kinds of exotic animals are available? Pet store workers should be able to tell you where all their animals come from. On your own, and with the help of an adult, go online to see if there are special rules in your community about owning any of the animals you saw at the store. For example, some cities have banned snakes larger than a certain size, but there are no restrictions on owning them as babies.

Kept captive, *exotic animals behave differently than they would in the wild. Some pet birds are so unhappy that they will pluck out their own feathers.*

ATTACK OF THE KILLER...GOLDFISH?

Brightly colored goldfish might seem like the most harmless pets in the world. But outside of bowls and ponds, these fish turn from pets to pests as an invasive aquatic, or water-dwelling, species.

Goldfish that have escaped from backyard ponds or been dumped in city waterways grow in size to 16 inches (41 cm) long. They can weigh up to 5 pounds (2.3 kg).

About 50 million goldfish live in Lake Ontario, eating fish, turtles, and frogs.

Goldfish thrive in cloudy, mucky ponds where the water is still.

Originally from China, goldfish swim in aquariums, ornamental, or decorative, ponds, and in the wild all over the globe.

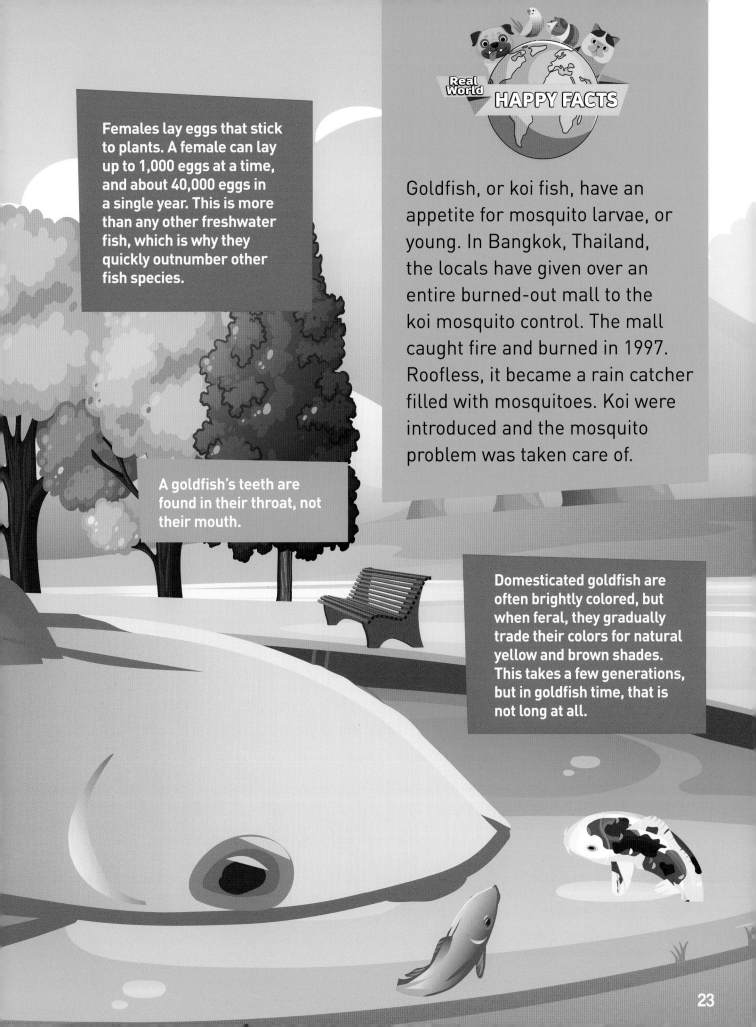

Females lay eggs that stick to plants. A female can lay up to 1,000 eggs at a time, and about 40,000 eggs in a single year. This is more than any other freshwater fish, which is why they quickly outnumber other fish species.

Goldfish, or koi fish, have an appetite for mosquito larvae, or young. In Bangkok, Thailand, the locals have given over an entire burned-out mall to the koi mosquito control. The mall caught fire and burned in 1997. Roofless, it became a rain catcher filled with mosquitoes. Koi were introduced and the mosquito problem was taken care of.

A goldfish's teeth are found in their throat, not their mouth.

Domesticated goldfish are often brightly colored, but when feral, they gradually trade their colors for natural yellow and brown shades. This takes a few generations, but in goldfish time, that is not long at all.

INVADERS AND GRAZERS

In many areas of the world, humans and domesticated animals live side-by-side. Humans benefit from this close association. Sometimes, domesticated animals become a problem when humans neglect them or release them into the wild. This upsets the balance of nature, especially when their populations explode.

BUNNY TASK FORCE

The city of Juneau, Alaska had a feral rabbit problem that it dealt with in a unique way. It formed its own Bunny Task Force. The task force included government agencies such as the Department of Fish and Game, animal control, the police, and the local Humane Society. It worked on a plan to ensure feral rabbits don't take over. The task force set up humane traps. Some bunnies were neutered or spayed, and some were put up for adoption. Others were humanely killed and their meat was donated to the American Bald Eagle Foundation. It was used to feed raptor birds.

Feral rabbit colonies can grow so quickly that they destroy the landscape by eating all of the vegetation.

The Black Mountains of Arizona are home to feral donkeys, called burros. They were abandoned by people looking for gold to mine. They compete with local wildlife, such as wild cattle, for food and water, which are already limited in the desert.

Look Around You:
Backyard BioBlitz

A BioBlitz is an inventory, or a complete record or list, of living things in a certain area. During BioBlitzes, professional **ecologists** join with citizen scientists at one location for a certain amount of time (12 or 24 hours). They gather information and identify as many species as possible during that time. You can do your own mini-inventory of species in your backyard or local park. Grab a notepad, observe, and write down how many animals you see in a two hour period. Try it again at another time of day. Did you notice anything different?

PIGEON POWER

They roost, or sleep, on buildings or peck seeds in parks. Pigeons are one of the most common city birds. They are feral—the **descendants** of rock doves that roosted on sea cliffs. Pigeons were domesticated for meat, sport, and as pets.

Building owners and landlords may place spikes on building ledges and rooftops to try to discourage pigeons from nesting.

Pigeons mate for life and are great parents.

Pigeons love cities because the life is easy—meaning there is plenty of food.

Pigeons molt, or shed, their feathers two to three times a year. Fright molt is when a pigeon suddenly loses a clump of its feathers all at once. They do this to defend themselves and escape when they're being handled aggressively or attacked.

In cities, pigeons live in flocks of up to 500 birds, sharing nesting areas in abandoned buildings where they are safe from predators.

Pigeons have a special relationship with humans because they were the first birds humans domesticated. Records show that ancient peoples kept pigeons.

Pigeons eat just about anything, including seeds, stale bread, insects, spiders, and leftover food garbage from trash cans.

Pigeons bob their heads to stabilize, or steady, their vision. Pushing their heads forward also helps them to see how close they are to something.

There are an estimated 260 million pigeons in cities around the world.

Male pigeons dance to attract a mate. They puff up their feathers, then quickly strut toward the female, cooing over and over again. He will bow and turn as he gets closer to the female.

Pigeons can sometimes be seen riding subways in big cities.

FERALS AROUND THE WORLD

Whether brought to a new place for human use, abandoned by owners, or born feral, once-domesticated, now-wild animals can be found all over the world. For all, survival depends on how well they can adapt and get along with humans. If they disrupt the environment too much, they will be considered to be pests.

NOT A PET

In Japan, feral raccoons became a problem after pet dealers began importing raccoons from North America. The animals are not native to Japan. But people wanted raccoons as pets after a cartoon series called *Rascal the Raccoon* became popular. Many of these pets were abandoned and released when they proved too wild to handle. They quickly adapted. Now, feral raccoons are fond of nesting in ancient wooden temples and are devouring food crops.

The Rascal the Raccoon show made people think raccoons could be cute and cuddly pets.

STREET DOG SMARTS

Street dogs are common in many cities of the world. They survive by being swift and smart. In Bucharest, Romania, street dogs have learned to obey traffic signals by watching people at rush hour. That's right, these dogs have taught themselves how to cross the street safely! Animal welfare charities, such as Four Paws, work to ensure the safety of stray animals in cities around the world. They check on animal health through mobile clinics. Four Paws also neuters and spays feral dogs in Romania, Bulgaria, and Ukraine.

Parakeet Pals

Sometimes, non-native ferals can fit in with their new **habitats**. Two red-masked parakeets escaped their homes in San Francisco around 1990. Far from their native countries of Peru and Ecuador, and without their owners to feed them, it seemed unlikely that the pair would survive. Surprisingly, the birds adjusted to the Telegraph Hill neighborhood. Other escaped parakeets joined them, and within 15 years, the flock had grown to 200 feral birds.

Street dogs in Bucharest, Romania have learned to cross busy roads at red lights. They learned how by watching humans do it.

29

LEARNING MORE

Books

Jacobs, Pat. *Cat Pals*. Crabtree Publishing, 2018.

Kalman, Bobbie. *Animals that Live in Social Groups*. Crabtree Publishing, 2016.

Laidlaw, Rob. *Saving Lives and Changing Hearts: Animal Sanctuaries and Rescue Centers*. Pajama Press, 2013.

Spelman, Lucy. *National Geographic Animal Encyclopedia*. National Geographic. 2012.

Websites

www.humanesociety.org
This website includes information on how to provide a humane backyard for wildlife.

www.humanecanada.ca
This organization helps educate people on animal welfare and works for better laws to protect animals.

https://kids.nationalgeographic.com/animals/
Learn about many different types of mammals, birds, reptiles, amphibians, invertebrates, and fish on this informative website.

www.coolkidfacts.com/animals/
Discover amazing facts about many types of animals on this cool website.

GLOSSARY

adapted Changed or became used to new conditions

animal sanctuary A place where animals can be safe

breeding Pairing animals to have babies

captive Confined, or not in the wild

conservation Protecting and preserving something so it survives in the future

descendants Developed or coming from a specific animal that lived previously

domesticated Animals that are tame or live closely with humans

ecologists Scientists who study living things and their physical surroundings

ecosystem A large community of plants, animals and other living things that live in a particular area

endangered At risk of extinction or being wiped out

glands Organs in an animal's body that release substances that serve a specific function, such as helping it grow

habitats The natural environment of a living thing, or the place where they are usually found living

heritage species A protected or rare species

humanely Done in a manner that causes the least amount of harm to an animal

mites Tiny or microscopic spider-like animals that live on and feed off plants and animals

native Belonging to, or originating in, a specific area

navigating Finding a way to travel over land, air, or water in the correct direction

neutered Describes a male animal that has been prevented from making babies

nocturnal Active at night

nuisance An animal that is bothersome and causes offence, especially under the law

originate To begin or start in a specific place

parasite Something that lives on another living thing, or host, often feeding off the host

predators Animals that kill other animals for food

prey An animal hunted for food by another animal

rangeland Land where animals forage and hunt for food

rehabilitated Restored to good health or condition

roadkill The body of an animal killed on a road by a moving vehicle

sow An adult female swine or pig

spayed Describes a female animal that has been prevented from making babies

species A group of living things that are related to each other

submissiveness Ready to yield to another's authority or control

urban Related to a city or town

vaccinated Given shots to be protected against a disease or disorder

INDEX

abandoned animals 4, 6, 13, 15, 25, 28

BioBlitzes 25

Bunny Task Force 24

Burmese pythons 20

burros 17, 24

cats 4, 6, 7, 8, 9, 12, 14, 15, 16, 17, 24

diseases 4, 9, 11, 14, 15

dogs 4, 6, 7, 8, 9, 13, 14–15

domesticated animals 4, 5, 17, 19, 23, 24, 26, 27, 28

escaped animals 4, 7, 13, 19, 20, 22, 29

euthanization 5

Everglades National Park 20

feral animals 4, 6, 8, 9, 12, 14, 15, 16, 17, 18–19, 24

goldfish 22–23

guinea pigs 12–13

hogs 16, 18–19

Humane Society 5, 6

invasive species 13, 20, 22, 25

mange 9

neutering and spaying 11, 12, 24, 29

nuisance animals 9

pigeons 26–27

rabbits 24

reptiles 7, 20

strays 4, 6, 7, 8, 9, 12, 14, 15, 29

street dogs 13

wild horses 17

QUESTIONS & ANSWERS

Q: Can I feed a feral animal?

A: Some cities or towns have laws against feeding feral animals—including pigeons. You should check with your city and your local Humane Society or ASPCA before caring for any feral.

Q: Can I adopt a feral animal?

A: It is not a good idea to take in a feral animal. If you are interested in adopting a pet, visit an animal shelter.